Family Scrapbook

School Life
in the 1940s and 50s

Faye Gardner with Anne Richardson

Evans

Published by in 2005 by Evans Brothers Limited
2A Portman Mansions
Chiltern St
London W1U 6NR

British Cataloguing in Publication Data
Gardner, Faye
School Life in Grandma's Day
1.Education, Elementary – Great Britain – History – 20th century – Juvenile literature
2.Great Britain – Social conditions – 20th century – Juvenile literature
I. Title
II. Richardson, Anne
372.9'42'09044

ISBN 0 237 53053 8
13 digit ISBN (from January 2007) 978 0 237 53053 2

© Evans Brothers Limited 1997
First published in paperback in 1998. Reprinted 1999, 2000, 2002 twice)

Acknowledgements
Planning and production by Discovery Books Limited
Edited by Faye Gardner
Designed by Ian Winton
Commissioned photography by Gerry McKann and Morris Nessam
Illustrations by Stuart Lafford

The publisher would like to thank Anne Richardson for her kind help in the preparation of this book.

For permission to reproduce copyright material, the author and publishers gratefully acknowledge
the following: Beamish, The North of England Open Air Museum, County Durham: cover (front, bottom
left), 9 (bottom right), 10, 11 (top), 12 (centre), 14, 17 (bottom), 18, 22 (top); Durham Record Office:
7 (centre); Hulton Getty: 16 (bottom), 19 (top), 20 (bottom), 21, 26; Olive Linge: 7 (top);
Topham Picturepoint: 9 (centre left), 22 (bottom), 23.

CONTENTS

My name is Anne and I am a grandmother. I have one grandson, Robbie, who is two and a half years old.

I was born in 1942 during the Second World War. When I was young I lived in a village called Willington, which is in the north of England.

The village was built around a big coal pit. You can see the pile of coal **slag** in this picture. My father was a coal miner and my mother was a housewife. All my friends' dads were miners, too.

I started school when I was five years old, two years after the war had ended. I am going to tell you about my school and how things were different for school children in those days.

'The schools were built in 1879.'

My first school was called Willington Infants. When I was seven I moved to the junior school, which was next door to the infants. The schools were built in 1879, out of red brick made in the village. They had the date they were built written on them.

Each school had its own headmaster. You can see my junior school headmaster in this picture. I am sitting near him in the second row. He lived in a house next to the school. There was a beautiful garden where we sometimes had gardening lessons.

Boys and girls had separate entrances to each school. Each entrance had GIRLS or BOYS carved above the door in stone. Every morning a teacher stood at each entrance to make sure that we used the right one.

There were nearly fifty children in my class! We sat in pairs behind wooden desks. The desks had lids and space inside for us to keep our books and pens. The teacher had her own desk at the front of the class.

During lessons we weren't allowed to move from our seats. When we finished our work, we put up a hand and waited for the teacher to come to our desk.

The walls of my classroom were bare apart from one or two charts like these, and a large blackboard. The room was heated by an open fire at the front of the class. If you were in the back row it didn't keep you very warm! The fire was looked after by the **caretaker**. Every couple of hours he came to put on more coal, which he carried in a large metal bucket.

My school had a big hall where we had PE lessons and put on a play each year.

Here I am with my class, in a play called *The Fairies of Bluebell Wood.*

11

'Teachers were very strict.'

Teachers were very strict and most classwork had to be done in silence. Anyone caught talking was punished straight away. In those days teachers used to smack children across the hands with a cane or a leather strap like these. It was very painful! Teachers often punished children for being lazy or for making mistakes in their work, too.

This is a photo of one of my teachers. Her name was Miss Tunstall. All of my teachers were women. During the war many male teachers had left their jobs to join the **armed forces**. None of my teachers was married because women teachers weren't allowed to get married in those days.

My favourite teacher was called Miss Walls. She had lots of pet animals and sometimes brought them to school to show her pupils. In this photo you can see her with her pet dog.

This photo was taken in May 1950. Willington football team had just won a cup and the goal keeper brought it to my school to have a picture taken. You can see the cup in the front of the photo and the goal keeper at the back. I'm sitting near the cup in the second row.

'We wrote with steel-nibbed pens.'

School started with a half-hour **assembly** in the hall. We had to sit cross-legged on the floor while the headmaster read out a story from the Bible. Afterwards we stood to say prayers, a teacher played the piano and we sang hymns.

Every morning we had lessons in sums, reading and handwriting. We wrote with steel-nibbed pens which had to be dipped in ink. It was much messier than writing with a ball-point pen! The **nibs** were scratchy and made splodges of ink on the paper.

During handwriting lessons we wrote in exercise books like this one. We had to fit letters between the lines on the page neatly. It took a lot of concentration!

I kept my pens in a wooden pencil box made by my grandad. It had a sliding top like this one, but my box also had a little compartment to keep new nibs.

'We had top and whip races.'

At playtime we went outside to play in the playground. There was always a teacher on duty. We played hopscotch with an old tobacco tin filled with pebbles. Some children collected picture cards from cigarette packets and brought them to school to swap with friends.

Sometimes we had top and whip races. A top was a little toy that looked like this. The whip was made of string or leather.

To start the top spinning you wrapped the whip around the top and pulled it away really quickly. You kept the top spinning by hitting it with the whip. The person who made their top spin the furthest was the winner.

When playtime was finished, the teacher rang a bell and we had to get into lines and walk back to class quietly.

'We didn't have many books.'

In those days schools didn't have computers or televisions. Some schools had **wireless** sets and children often listened to radio programmes as part of their lessons.

At my school we had a jumble sale to make money to buy a wireless. It took a whole year to collect enough things for the sale, and we made a total of £70. That was a lot of money in those days!

We didn't have many books so we had to copy things off the blackboard and learn them by heart. During reading lessons we had to share one book between the whole class! Each pupil had to read a few lines aloud then pass the book to the next person.

We read adventure stories like *The Arabian Nights*, *Peter Pan*, and *Robin Hood And His Merry Men*.

'Children got a free drink of milk.'

In those days most people were less well off than they are now. At my school we didn't have to wear uniforms because most children couldn't afford them. Here I am wearing a jumper that my mum knitted out of wool unpicked from old jumpers.

The government tried to help children by giving them free school dinners.

For many children school dinners were the only hot meal they would get that day! The dinners were cooked in a big kitchen at the school. We usually had meat

and mashed potato, with jam sponge for pudding.

Children got a free drink of milk at school, too. The milk came in 1/3 pint bottles (less than a quarter litre), with straws stuck in

the top. The caretaker brought the bottles to our classroom in big wooden crates. When we finished our milk we put the empty bottles back in the crates for the caretaker to take away.

'We learned about the British Empire.'

Most afternoons we had lessons in geography or history. In geography we learned about the countries of the **British Empire** and Europe. We used a globe, like this one, to learn the names of the capital cities and main rivers of each country by heart.

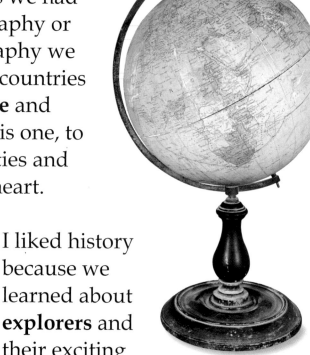

I liked history because we learned about **explorers** and their exciting journeys. When I was eleven, we did a project on two explorers called Edmund Hillary and Tenzing Norgay. They had just climbed to the top of Mount Everest, the highest mountain in the world.

Every Friday the teacher gave us a test on everything we had learned that week.

Three times a week we had PE. The lessons were in the hall because we didn't have a playing field. There wasn't much sports equipment. We spent most of the lesson doing exercises and jumping on the spot.

When I was young every child had to take an exam called the 11 Plus in their last year at junior school. If you passed the 11 Plus exam, you could go to a grammar school. I went to grammar school in a town near my village called Wolsingham.

The photo above shows the old entrance to the school. The writing on the bricks tells you the school first opened in 1614!

At grammar school we had to wear navy uniforms and the teachers wore long, black gowns and flat, square hats called mortar boards. The photo below was taken during my last year at grammar school. I'm in the front row, on the left.

Before the war, most children left school at fourteen to get a job. After the war, the government made a new rule which said children had to go to school until they were fifteen years old.

'Children were given school prizes.'

At grammar school we studied subjects we had never learned before like French, cookery and science. My favourite subject was chemistry.

Each subject was taught in a different classroom so we moved about quite a lot. The classrooms had tables instead of desks so we had to carry our books around in satchels.

At the end of each term we had exams in every subject. The results were written in report books which we had to take home to our parents.

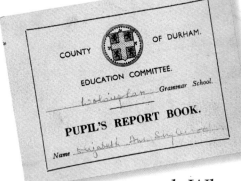

This report says I've had too many days off school and I need to work harder!

Children who got high marks were sometimes given school prizes as a reward. When I was fifteen I won a book for getting top marks in science.

My grammar school had its own magazine called *The Phoenix*, which was written by pupils at the school.

THE PHOENIX
WOLSINGHAM GRAMMAR SCHOOL MAGAZINE

School time wasn't just about doing lessons and exams: we had time to enjoy ourselves, too.

This is a picture of me at my sixth birthday party with some of my friends from school.

Here I am having fun in a school play with some girls from my class.

GLOSSARY

Armed forces The army, navy or airforce.

Assembly When all the pupils and teachers in a school come together, usually to sing songs and say a prayer.

British Empire A group of countries that used to be ruled by Britain, like India and parts of Africa.

Caretaker A person who looks after the school buildings.

Explorer A person who travels to parts of the world to find out more about the land, the people and wildlife that live there.

Nib The metal point of a pen.

Slag The waste from a coal mine.

Wireless A radio.

OTHER BOOKS TO READ

Other books about twentieth-century history for younger readers published by Evans include:

Rainbows *When Grandma Was Young*
Rainbows *When Dad Was Young*
Rainbows *What Was It Like Before Television?*
Tell Me About *Emmeline Pankhurst*
Tell Me About *Enid Blyton*

Britain Through The Ages *Britain Since 1930*
Alpha *1960s*
Take Ten Years *1930s, 1940s, 1950s, 1960s, 1970s, 1980s*

INDEX